Introduction to
Simple Sewing
Home Accessories

igloobooks

Published in 2015
by Igloo Books Ltd
Cottage Farm
Sywell
NN6 0BJ
www.igloobooks.com

Cover images © Thinkstock / Getty Images

LEO002 1015
2 4 6 8 10 9 7 5 3
ISBN 978-1-78440-325-6

Printed and manufactured in China

Introduction to
Simple
Sewing
Home Accessories

Contents

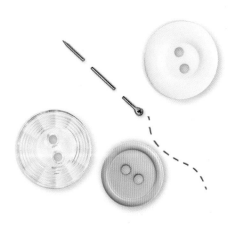

Introduction

Follow the step-by-step sewing instructions
in this comprehensive how-to guide and
learn to create your own stylish garments,
fun accessories and charming homewares.

Needles

All you ever wanted to know about sewing machine needles but were afraid to ask!

A common mistake often made by beginners is to use the same needle for everything you sew. The size of the needle that you need for a specific job depends on the size of the fabric yarns in the fabric you are sewing. For example, if you are sewing a fine fabric, you need to use a fine needle, which must be fine enough not to mark the fabric and yet still have a big enough eye to ensure that the thread does not break or fray while you are sewing with it.

With so many different needles out there, all with seemingly bewildering names, how do you know which one to choose?

Sharp points (regular)

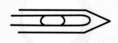

For use with woven fabrics because they cause a minimum amount of puckering and produce an even stitch without damaging the fabric. They are not recommended for use with knits because they can cause skipped stitches.

Sharp points are more slender through the shaft and should be used when edge stitching on woven fabrics, sewing on finely woven fabrics or heirloom stitching very fine fabrics. They are also a good choice when sewing with synthetic suede. These needles come in varying sizes from the finest size 9 to the heaviest size 18.

Ball-point needles

Specifically designed to be used with knitted and stretchy fabrics. Ball-point needles have a rounded point rather than a sharp one so they push between the fabric yarns rather than piercing them the way the sharp points do. This eliminates any potential damage to knitted fabrics.

These needles should be used when sewing with interlock knits, coarse knits and other fabrics that will run if snagged. The needles come in varying sizes from 9 to 16. The larger the size of the needle, the more rounded the needle point is.

Wedge-point needles

Designed for use with leather and vinyl, these needles will easily pierce these fabrics and create a hole that will close back up on itself. The wedge shape makes it a superior needle for piercing tough, unyielding fabrics, such as leather or suede. However, if you're sewing synthetic leathers or suede, it's better to use a standard needle because a wedge point needle will leave a large hole and weaken the seam.

These needles come in varying sizes from 11 to 18. The smaller sizes are suitable for softer, more pliable leather, while the larger sizes are designed for sewing heavy leathers, or multiple layers.

Embroidery needles

These have a larger eye to accommodate the thicker embroidery threads. They also have a special scarf (the groove above the eye) that protects decorative threads from breaking.

...e size of the needle
...at you need for a
...ecific job depends on
...e size of the fabric
...rns in the fabric you
...e sewing."

Quilting needles

...so called Betweens, these have a
...pered point that allows you to stitch
...rough more layers of fabric (usually the
...ilt sandwich) and across intersecting
...ams. The tapered point prevents damage
...pricey, heirloom-quality fabrics.
...ey are usually smaller and stronger
...an regular needles with a small eye,
...d come in sizes 9 (largest) to 12.

Universal-point needles

...ave a slightly rounded point, similar to
...e ball-point needle, and are used for
...eneral, everyday sewing of woven or
...nitted fabrics. The needle is tapered so
...slips through the fabric weave of the
...nit easily while still retaining enough
...harpness to pierce the cloth. They come
... many different sizes with 14/90 and
...1/75 being the most popular.

Size of Needle

Once you know which is the right type of needle to use for a sewing project, it's important to know which size of needle to use. Although there are exceptions, as a general rule, the needle size is judged by the type of fabric being sewn.

MEDIUM-WEIGHT FABRICS

If sewing with slightly heavier weight fabrics such as gingham, poplin, linen, muslin, chambray, wool crepe, flannel, knits, jersey, wool, wool suiting or stretch fabrics, a size 14 needle is generally best.

LIGHTWEIGHT FABRICS

When using lighter weight fabrics such as synthetic sheers, batiste, taffeta or velvet, a size 11 needle would be the normal choice.

MEDIUM-HEAVY FABRICS

Sewing with fabrics such as gabardine, heavy suiting or tweed would require a size 16 needle.

HEAVY FABRICS

When using heavy-weight fabrics such as denim, ticking, upholstery or canvas, a size 18 needle is the most suitable.

DELICATE FABRICS

When sewing with extremely delicate fabrics such as silk, chiffon, voile, fine lace or organza, a fine size 9 needle would usually be the best choice.

Main image:
Invest in a variety of needles that are easy to keep organised – many packs also offer advice on which needle is best for which fabric.

Always replace a dull or damaged needle straight away. Damaged needles can cause skipped stitches and tearing of your fabric."

Fabric Types

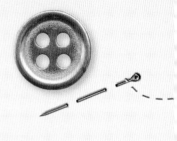

Do you know your burlap from your chintz, or moleskin from ticking? Here's our brief guide to the most common fabrics.

Brocade

A dense weave with the appearance of all-over embroidery. The silk version is most often used for formal wear, while you'll find the cotton version for upholstery.

Burlap/Hessian

Often woven from hemp, jute or raw cotton, it's best used for curtains, wall hangings and sacks. It's also a great base for embroidery.

Calico

A light cotton fabric used for children's clothes and home furnishings.

Candlewick

Famous for bedspreads, this tufted fabric is thick and soft.

Canvas

A heavy fabric that's most often made from cotton, but is sometimes made of a blend of natural and synthetic materials.

Cheesecloth

A lovely lightweight, loosely woven cotton fabric. Used for summer-weight tops and dresses, although as the name suggests, it was originally used in the production of cheese.

Chiffon

Made from silk or polyester, this formal wear fabric is light with a good drape. It works well for multi-layered garments, and for those with tucks and gathers. Use a fine needle to construct the seams.

Chintz

This most often floral-printed fabric is used for heavyweight curtains and upholstery. Synonymous with the English country cottage look.

Cotton

Comes from the seed pod of the cotton plant. It forms the basis for a plethora of fabrics, on its own in muslins and canvas, or spun with polyester.

Corduroy

A fabric with a rib effect, usually cut with the stripes falling vertically. Available in different weights – the heavier the weight, the wider the ribs.

Crêpe

Woven with a twist in the fibres, this fabric has an almost creased look to it. Sometimes it is backed with satin.

Crêpe de Chine

Mostly made from synthetic fibres rather than the traditional silk, this lightweight, plain-weave fabric is used for evening wear and blouses.

Damask

A firm weave of cotton, linen or blends, often forming a pattern with metallic or reflective areas. Often used for interiors, particularly table linen and bedding.

Denim

Famously strong fabric originally used for work clothes, now worn by everyone, whether for work or pleasure. Made with coloured warp and white weft. Use a denim-specific needle with a heavy cotton thread.

Drill

Similar to denim, this strong weave is made from cotton. There is usually a strong bias (diagonal) in the weave.

Felt

A wool fabric made by agitation and rubbing of the wet fibres; the application of heat fixes it. A great fabric for children learning to sew.

Flannel

Soft, pliable fabric made from wool or cotton blends. Always pre-wash flannel before working with it because it can shrink, but it can also stretch when worn. It's a good idea to add a little to the seam allowance because it has a tendency to fray.

Gabardine

A heavyweight woven twill that is the main fabric for raincoats and sportswear.

Gingham

Cute cotton fabric, woven to give an almost chequerboard effect. Used for cottage-style interiors and children's clothes.

Always pre-wash flannel before working with it because it can shrink, but it can also stretch when worn."

Jacquard

Named after its inventor, Joseph Jacquard, this heavy fabric is woven on looms, with a raised surface and often with images. You'll find this fabric adorning upholstery in many stately homes.

Jersey

A common name given to 'knitted' versatile fabrics. Has a tendency to stretch width wise. It's best to hem jersey with a twin needle to top stitch.

Lamé

This name is given to fabrics that are woven with metallic fibres.

Linen

The fibres of the stalks of the flax plant are used to make this fabric. It's known for creasing heavily but it's possible to purchase some linens that have been blended with synthetic fibres that crease less. For best results, sew using a cotton thread with 9–12 stitches per inch.

Moleskin

No moles are killed in the making of this heavy fabric. It's actually cotton based, which is then brushed to create a suede-like quality.

Muslin

A cotton weave that comes in various qualities. Dressmakers like to used it to make 'dummy' garments before cutting the actual, intended material to size.

Net

Most often made from nylon, this open, knotted fabric has hexagonal-shaped holes.

Polyester

A product of the petro-chemical industry, this fibre can take on the appearance of silk, blend with other fibres, or be turned into batting for quilts and stuffing for toys.

Satin

Not exactly a fabric type, but the name given to a particular weave of silk, cotton and polyester. Needle and pin marks will show on satin, so check all measurements before sewing. It's also a good idea to change your needle regularly to avoid it snagging.

Shot Silk

This is the effect achieved when the weft and the warp of the weave are different colours. As the fabric moves, it appears to change colour.

Silk

Comes from unwinding the cocoon of the silk worm. It's a strong yet delicate fibre, and has been discovered as being used over 5,000 years ago in China.

Taffeta

Made from cotton, polyester or silk, this fabric has a subtle sheen but it also rustles when it moves.

Ticking

The most common use for this fabric is pillowcases. It's recognisable by its white/cream background with blue stripes.

Tweed

Woven from pure wool, often with slubs of another shade running though it. Its hard-wearing nature makes it the perfect fabric for making suits.

Velvet

A weave with a short-cut fibre, traditionally made from silk fibre, but nowadays also woven from synthetics.

CHOOSING
Thread

There are many different types of sewing thread that should all be used for different projects. Join us in investigating some of the most commonly used ones.

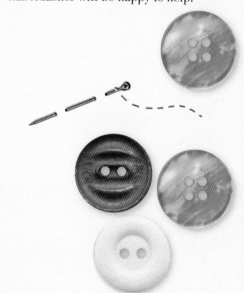

The type of thread that you use when sewing a particular project will be chosen based on the type of fabric you are using, and the project that you are sewing.

There are many different types of thread available to buy, but we are going to look at ones that you are most likely to use with your sewing machine. Thread comes in different thicknesses; general purpose threads tend to be medium thickness of about size 50. Cotton is the most commonly used thread and is available in a huge array of colours. You are most likely to use cotton thread if you are sewing linen, rayon or medium-weight cottons.

Most cotton threads are mercerized, which means that the thread is smooth and shiny. It is not advisable to use cotton thread for sewing on jersey projects, as the jersey fabric is very stretchy and cotton has no stretch.

Fine silk threads are most often used for sewing on silk and wool. The make up of this thread gives it quite elastic qualities, meaning that it can be used on jersey fabrics with some success. Silk threads are also idea for basting stitches because they are very fine and so will not leave holes when you remove the stitches at the end of the project.

Alternatives

You also have the choice of using nylon or polyester threads when sewing light to medium-weight fabrics. Polyester is good for using on stretch fabrics, as well as knitted and woven fabrics. Many polyester sewing threads will be coated with silicone to minimize friction as you are sewing with them, allowing them to freely flow through your machine. Another alternative to cotton/polyester threads is a hybrid of the two. Cotton wrapped polyester gives you the best of both types of thread. It is strong and elastic with a tough, heat-resistant surface.

Cotton, polyester and the cotton wrapped polyester are also available in heavier weights and are most suitable for sewing upholstery fabrics or heavier weights of clothing. If you are unsure which thread is best for your fabric, your local haberdasher will be happy to help.

"The type of thread you use in your next sewing project will depend upon the type of fabric that you are going to be sewing."

Basic Stitches

There are lots of different stitches that you can use to create a range of effects in your sewing projects.
The ones on these pages are some of the most popular.

Chain Stitch If you want to create thick, pretty lines quickly, this is the stitch to use.

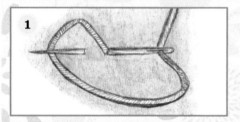 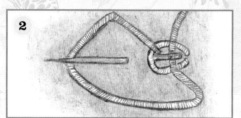 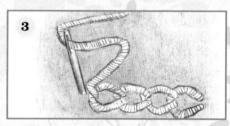

Step 1

Pull the needle to the right side where you want your chain-stitch line to start. Insert the needle close to where you brought it up and, without pulling it through, bring the needle up approx. 0.5cm (¼in) along the line, looping the thread under the point. Pull the needle through and tease the stitch to make it even.

Step 2

Now push the needle back through the fabric, very close to where it came up in the loop, and bring it up 0.5cm (¼in) along the line you are following. Loop the thread under the point of the needle again and pull the needle through, again teasing the stitch to even it out.

Step 3

Repeat step two until you have a length of chain stitches. Keep the stitches even by leaving the same 0.5cm (¼in) gap and teasing out each stitch as you go. Don't pull too hard on the thread as the fabric may pucker. To finish, secure the last loop with a little stitch at the top of the curve.

Split Stitch Perfect for making curved lines, flower stems and outline stitches.

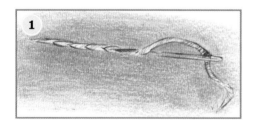 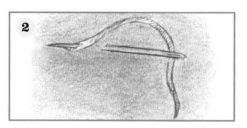

Step 1

It's best to work from left to right. Start by bringing the needle through to the right side, at the point where your line begins. Take the needle down a stitch to the right, then bring it up halfway along the previous stitch, splitting the thread.

Step 2

Place the next stitch to the right of the first, taking the needle back up through the previous stitch as before. Continue in this manner until your line is finished.

"Be careful when pressing embroidery with an iron, you could flatten the stitches."

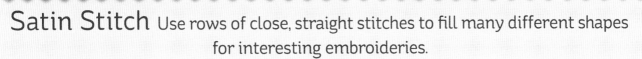

Satin Stitch Use rows of close, straight stitches to fill many different shapes for interesting embroideries.

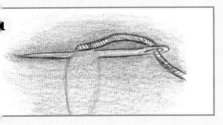
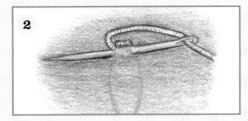
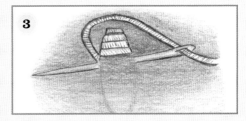

ep 1

ou are unsure about working freehand, e a fading marker pen to mark out your sign. Starting at one side, at the top of r shape, bring the thread through to the ht side and back down on the opposite ge of your design. Bring the needle up xt to where you first brought the thread ough.

Step 2

Insert the needle back through to the wrong side, close to where you made the first stitch, then bring it back up through on the opposite side of the shape. Don't pull too tight or the shape will distort.

Step 3

Continue making these parallel stitches, from one side of the shape to the other, until your shape is full. Fasten off the thread at the back of your work.

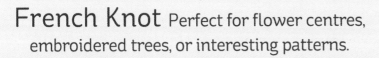

French Knot Perfect for flower centres, embroidered trees, or interesting patterns.

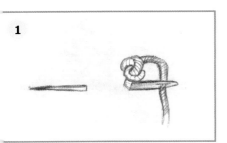

Step 1

Pull the needle through to the right side where you want the knot positioned. Wind the thread twice around the needle and insert the needle very close to where the thread came through to the right side.

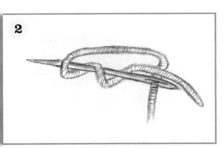

Step 2

Holding the stitch with the thumb, pull the needle through to the wrong side and secure the thread, or bring it through to the right side where you want to place another knot.

Satin Stitch Use rows of close, straight stitches to fill many different shapes for interesting embroideries.

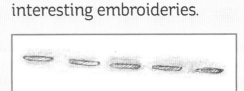

Step 1

Lay a line of running stitches along the line that you want to sew and fasten off. Now choose another colour of thread or keep the same thread, and change to a blunt-ended darning needle, depending on the size of your running stitches.

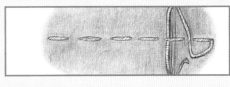

Step 2

Starting at one end of your running stitch line, bring the needle through to the right side, close to the start of the first stitch. Using the blunt end of your needle, weave the thread through your foundation line of stitches, taking care not to pull too tightly.

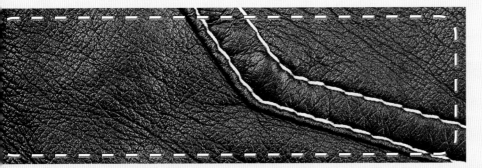

Basic Stitches

Once you have mastered the basic stitches you can add extra detail to garments with more decorative techniques.
Here are a few more stitches to increase your sewing repertoire.

Lazy Dazy Sometimes called the 'detached chain stitch', you'll most often find it used to make flowers due to the petal shape. Perfect for a quick embellishment.

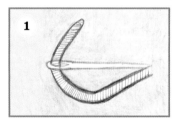
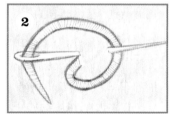
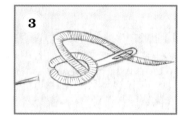
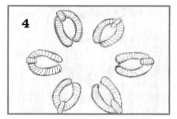

Step 1

Mark on the fabric with a fading marker where you want the stitches placed. Now bring the needle and thread through to the right side at the base of the stitch position. Take the needle down again, very close to this, but don't pull the thread through.

Step 2

Bring the tip of the needle to right side of the fabric to the length that you want your 'petal' to be, making sure the needle point goes over the thread loop, and pull through.

Step 3

Take the needle back down to make a small securing stitch and adjust the loop to the shape desired.

Step 4

You can group the stitches together to make a flower formation, or add them to a stem-stitched line to give the look of leaves on a stem.

Bullion Knots Wind the thread around your needle, to create these effective, large knots.

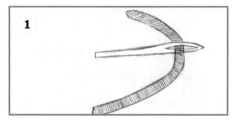
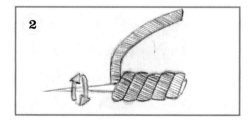
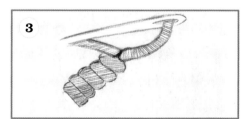

Step 1

Bring the needle up through the fabric where you want to place the stitch and take it back down the same distance that you want the knot to be, but don't pull the thread all the way through.

Step 2

Bring the needle and thread up at the first position and wind the thread from the first stitch around the point by rotating the needle around the thread.

Step 3

Hold the wound thread close to the fabric with the thumb of your other hand and gently pull the needle and thread through. Take the needle down at the other end of the stitch to secure.

Laid Trailing Stitch
Make short stitches over a thread of the same colour for a 3D feel.

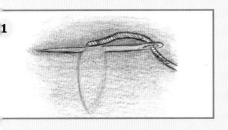 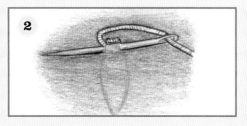 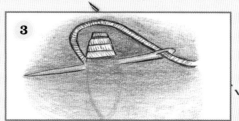

Step 1
...ke your needle through to the wrong ...e of your fabric where you want the line ...start, leaving a tail end that is the same ...gth as the line you are creating. Place ...loose thread over your work, roughly in ...pattern you want to embroider.

Step 2
Bring the needle up, close to the start of the line. Now take the needle down on the other side of the tail thread and pick up a small bit of fabric beneath the loose thread (as if to encompass the thread).

Step 3
The next and all consecutive stitches should be placed close to the previous one. Continue in this manner until the length of the tail thread has been covered.

Long and Short Stitch
Use this technique to fill in large areas of your embroidery.

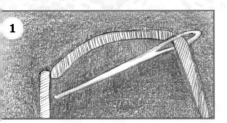 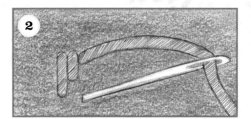 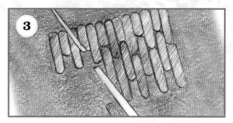

Step 1
...ring the needle up through the fabric ...here you want to place the stitch and ...ke it back down the same distance that ...ou want the knot to be, but don't pull ...e thread all the way through.

Step 2
Bring the needle and thread up at the first position and wind the thread from the first stitch around the point by rotating the needle around the thread.

Step 3
Hold the wound thread close to the fabric with the thumb of your other hand and gently pull the needle and thread through. Take the needle down at the other end of the stitch to secure.

Stem Stitch
By placing short stitches close to each other you can create flowing lines. Great for embroidering swirls, flower stems and other abstract shapes.

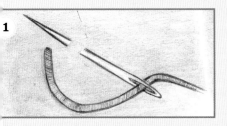 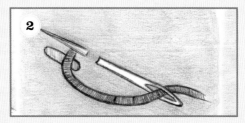 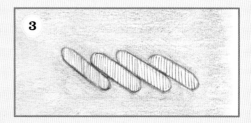

Step 1
...s best work this stitch from left to right. ...ing the thread through the fabric where ...want the line to start. Then push the ...edle through to the stitch width, and up ...ain halfway along and to the side the ...st stitch length.

Step 2
Push the needle through for the next stitch width and bring it up halfway along and to the side of the previous stitch as you did in step 1.

Step 3
Continue making stitches in this way until you have filled the area needed.

SEWING
TERMS

Our quick reference guide to the sewing terminology that you'll find on the patterns.

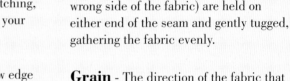

Appliqué - Sewing a piece of fabric on top of another for decorative reasons. When done by machine, a satin stitch (tight zigzag) is often used.

Backstitching - Sewing back and forth over the same stitches to lock the end or the beginning of a line of sewing.

Batting - The filling in a quilt. It can be fiberfill, cotton, wool or other material that is flattened and usually bought by the metre or yard. It is the middle of the quilt sandwich. Also known as wadding.

Bias - Runs diagonally to the straight grain of the fabric. Fabric cut on the bias has more stretch

Basting - The sewing of a temporary stitch. The stitches are large so as to be easily removed. They can be sewn by hand or machine but always with a view to being able to remove them easily.

Binding - Encasing the raw edges of a blanket or quilt with another piece of fabric. Binding can be bought pre-made or made yourself.

Blanket Stitch - A hand or machine stitch that is used to neaten the edge of a blanket, buttonhole or other seam line.

Casing - An envelope of sorts, usually along a waistline or a cuff, which encases elastic or drawstrings, etc.

Darn - To repair a hole by using stitches going back and forth that fill the hole. Some sewing machines come with darning attachments and stitches, which can also be used for free-motion quilting.

Embellish - To add special stitching, appliqués or other decorations to your sewing project.

Facing - Fabric sewn on the raw edge of a garment piece, which is turned under and serves as a finish for the edge as well.

Fat Quarter - A quilting term that refers to the size of a piece of fabric. A fat quarter is ¼ yard of fabric, about 18in x 22in, as opposed to a regular ¼ yard, which is 9in x 45in.

Finish (an edge) - To turn under 0.5cm (¼in) and stitch or serge the edge so that it doesn't fray or have too much bulk.

Fuse - The use of a special material that melts to 'glue' two layers together. The fusing works by being melted with an iron.

Fusible Web - Is available in a variety of weights and sizes.

Gathering - A method of easing a seam to allow insertion of sleeves and other rounded pattern pieces. To gather the seam, two parallel lines are sewn on the right side of the fabric. Long tails of thread are left for gathering. The bobbin threads (on the wrong side of the fabric) are held on either end of the seam and gently tugged, gathering the fabric evenly.

Grain - The direction of the fabric that runs parallel to the selvedge.

Hem - An edge that is turned under to the inside of a sewn item, and sewn.

Interfacing - An unseen addition to various parts of a garment, which adds body that the fabric alone would not add. Interfacing is available in many weights, in woven, knitted and non-woven forms as well as fusible and sew-in forms.

Inseam - The seam on a trouser leg that runs from the crotch to the hem.

Mitre - A technique that gives a corner a smooth, tidy finish, neatly squaring the corners while creating a diagonal seam from the point of the corner to the inside edge. Often used for the corners of a quilt binding.

otion - A term used for any item used r sewing other than the fabric and the achine.

ressing - A different process from oning. Instead of running the iron across e fabric, you gently lift the iron to press a ew area so as not to distort the fabric grain.

aglan Sleeve - A type of sleeve that tends in one piece fully to the collar, aving a diagonal seam from armpit collarbone.

ight Side - The right side of the bric is the side that the design is on. ometimes a fabric has no discernible ght side, so then it is up to the sewer to ecide which is the right side.

otary Cutter - A cutting tool used quilting to cut fabric instead of scissors. haped like a pizza cutter, it is perfect for tting long strips of fabric or many layers once.

unning Stitch - A simple stitch that often used for basting or as the basis narking) for another, more decorative, itch.

erger - A type of sewing machine that itches the seam, encases the seam with read, and cuts off excess fabric at the me time. These are used for construction garments with knit fabrics mostly, or to nish seams of any fabric.

Seam Allowance - The area between the stitching and raw, cut edge of the fabric. The most common seam allowances are ¼in, ½in and 5/8in. Your pattern should say which seam allowance you are to use.

Selvedge - The edges of the fabric that has the manufacturer's information. The information on a selvedge may include colour dots in the order that the colours were printed on to the fabric and lines to indicate the repeat of the pattern printed on the fabric.

Straight Stitch - The regular stitch that most sewing machines make.

Top Stitch - A sometimes decorative, sometimes functional stitch that is usually ¼in from the edge of a seam.

Tension - There are two types of tension on your sewing machine - the thread and bobbin tensions.

Tack - To sew a few stitches in one spot, by hand or by machine sewing, to secure one item to another.

Wrong Side - The side of the fabric that has no design on it or that you don't want facing outwards. Sometimes there is no discernible wrong side to a fabric.

Zigzag Stitch - A stitch that goes one way and then the other and provides a nice finish to a seam to prevent fraying. It can also be used as a decorative stitch.

Home

Create some wonderful one-of-a-kind pieces for your home that are both useful and beautiful, with these exciting projects. Bring some home-made heart to your living space!

Retro Cushions

Using a plain piece of fabric and a few fat eighths, you can make some beautiful cushions.

About this Pattern

2 ○○○○○ Intermediate

Step 1
CUT STRIPS

For a cushion cover that will fit a 41cm (16in) cushion insert, cut a piece of fabric that is 46cm (18in) tall and 107cm (42in) wide. Measure 30cm (12in) in from each end, fold here and press so that you can see what will be the front of your cushion.

Step 2
MARK CENTRE OF CUSHION

Cut strips of fabric in different widths that are long enough to cover as much of the front of your cushion as you wish to have striped.

Step 3
SEW STRIPS

Sew the strips to the front of your cushion using a zigzag stitch. Overlap them if you wish and arrange them in a pleasing manner.

MATERIALS

5 fat eighths of co-ordinating fabrics
50cm (22½in) square of brown upholstery fabric for each cushion

A selection of buttons, if desired

Matching thread

Top Tip

For an alternative stripey look, try varying the width of your strips – how about using random strip sizes, or arranging narrow strips working up to wide strips.

Step 4
NEATEN EDGES

Sew a 1/3cm (½in) hem at either end of the rectangle of fabric that is going to be your cushion.

Step 5
SEW CUSHION

With right-sides facing up on a table, fold the left-hand side in and sew along the top and bottom edge. Repeat with the right hand side. The edges should overlap, giving you a pocket that you can put your cushion into when it is turned the right-side out.

STEP 6
FINISHING TOUCHES

Turn the cushion cover right-side out and stuff with a cushion pad. Hand sew on buttons, ribbon or your choice of finishing touches.

Flower cushion

Make as above. Cut some simple petal shapes and zigzag stitch in place on the front of your cushion. You could embellish the centre with buttons, felt or a smaller flower shape.

Button cushion

Make as above, but decorate by sewing a selection of small buttons to the front of your cushion, grouped in one corner for a chic effect.

Top Tip

These striking cushions would make a great gift for family or friends – or why not make one to give as a housewarming present?

Aromatic Door Stop

A fun and colourful approach to a practical household accessory. Add lavender or other dried herbs for a delicate scent.

Step 1
CUT TEMPLATE PIECES

Using the dimensions given on the cutting list or your own templates, cut out all the relevant pieces to make your door stop.

Step 2
PREPARE SIDES

Fold the exterior fabric in half width ways with the right sides together and sew down the side. Repeat with the interior fabric side but leave a 6cm (2 3/8in) gap for turning.

STEP 3
PREPARE BASE

Pin the exterior circle fabric to the exterior fabric base, right sides together and sew with a 0.5cm (2/8in) seam allowance. Repeat with the interior fabric pieces (Fig. 1).

Step 4
SEW TOGETHER

Place your exterior fabric bag inside the interior fabric bag, right sides together. Pin them in place and then stitch them together around the top (Fig. 2).

FINISHED SIZE
22cm x 15cm (8½in x 6in)

MATERIALS
Patterned exterior fabric
Patterned interior fabric
Plain cotton fabric for the inner bag
Thick garden twine - 2m (79in)
Toy stuffing - 50g
Rice (for filling) - 1.5kg - 2kg
Lavender scented buds - 50g

CUTTING LIST
FROM EXTERIOR FABRIC:
1 x 52cm x 30cm (20½in x 12in)
1 x circle - 15cm (6in) diameter
FROM INTERIOR FABRIC:
1 x 52cm x 30cm (20½in x 12in)
1 x circle - 15cm (6in) diameter
FROM PLAIN COTTON:
1 x 52cm x 30cm (20½in x 12in)
1 x circle - 15cm (6in) diameter

PATTERN NOTES
Seam allowances are 1cm (3/8) unless otherwise stated.

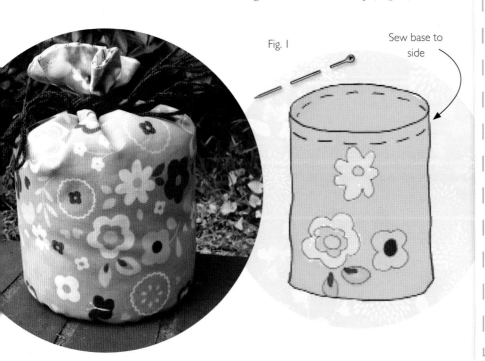

Fig. I

Sew base to side

"Make this door stop to any size using any circular template you have handy, such as a tea plate. Just make sure you adjust the side pieces accordingly."

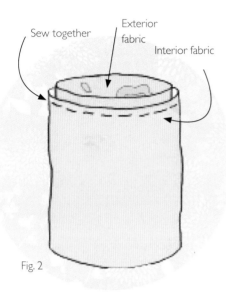

Sew together

Exterior fabric

Interior fabric

Fig. 2

Turn right-side out by pulling the exterior fabric bag out through the turning gap in the lining. Slip stitch the gap closed by hand and press to iron out any creases and make a neat edge. Top stitch around top edge for reinforcement working with right side uppermost and stitching about 6mm from the fabric edge.

Step 5
MAKE INNER BAG

Neaten one long edge of plain cotton by turning under 2cm (⁶/₈in) then tucking raw edge under again. Press and stitch in place close to inner fold. Sew the inner bag together as before and turn right side out. Fill with rice and lavender buds and tie it closed tightly with some twine.

Step 6
COMPLETE DOOR STOP

Place the rice bag inside the fabric bag and stuff the door stop with toy filling to give it more shape. Wind the twine around the top of the door stop as length allows and tie in place with a secure knot or bow (Fig. 3).
Your door stop is now ready to add a delicate fragrance and effortless style to your room.

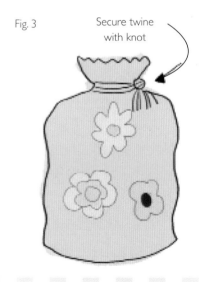

Fig. 3

Secure twine with knot

Colourful Storage

This storage dumpty is perfect for brightening up and tidying up any room.

About this Pattern

1 ●●○○○ Beginner

FABRIC

Motif fabric: approx 100cm x 100cm (40in x 40in)
Plain fabric for the outer strip: 40cm x 185cm (16in x 72in)

MATERIALS

Zip approx 48cm (19in)

PATTERN NOTES

We used a 1.5cm (⅝in) seam allowance

Step 1

CUT TWO CIRCLES

Cut out two circles to the size you want your storage dumpty to be. We cut out two large circular motifs from our fabric, each measuring 60cm (23in) in diameter. We formed one of these circles out of two incomplete circles that ran off the edge of the fabric. We joined this circle together with the zip that opens the storage dumpty.

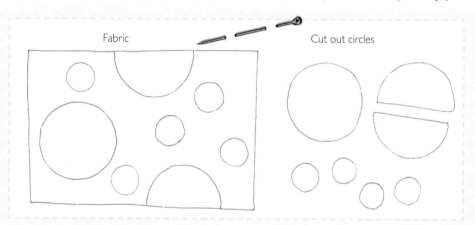

Fabric   Cut out circles

To do this, take one of your two incomplete circles (they need to be larger than semi-circles to allow for seaming) and position the zip along one straight edge, around 2cm (¾in) from the curved edge, right-sides to right-sides. Sew in place on the wrong-side, then fold and iron the seam over to the right-side. Now pin the other incomplete half circle on the other side of the zip, right-sides to right-sides, and check that the pattern on the circles lines up. Sew in place on the wrong-side, then fold and iron the seam over to the right-side.

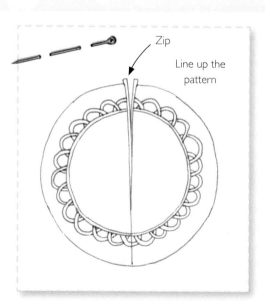

Zip

Line up the pattern

28

Step 2
CUT THE OUTER STRIP

The finished height of the dumpty will be 37cm (14.5in). Cut the outer strip piece to 40cm (15¾in), to allow for a 1.5cm (½in) seam.

For the circles, at 60cm (23½in) diameter, take off the seam allowance of 1.5cm (½in) on both edges, leaving 57.5cm (225/8in).

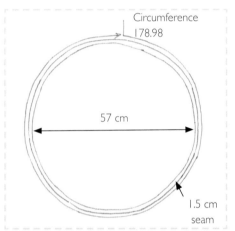

The circumference of a 57cm circle is 179cm (70½in). Add 6cm (2¼in) for the seam allowance, giving a total length for the outer strip of 185cm (73in).

Step 3
DECORATE OUTER STRIP

Next, cut out various shapes and sew them onto your outer strip. You can cut out other sizes of circles from the same fabric and zigzag stitched them onto the strip using red thread. You might wish to pin them or use a temporary adhesive so the shapes stay in place while you sew them on.

Step 4
SEW TOGETHER

Finally, pin the zip circle along one edge of the outer strip, right sides to right sides. Sew together, starting 4cm (1½in) from the end of the outer strip, all the way round

and stopping 4cm (1½in) before the end of the outer strip. Undo the zip and repeat with the other circle on the other side. You should have a small gap not sewn up along the circle edges.

Now pin in place the remaining gap along the circle edges and pin together the end edges of the outer strip.

Remove the pins along the circle edge and sew up the end edges of the outer strip. Iron the seam to one side and re-pin the circle edge and sew up the gap, while also catching down the edges of the side seam.

Step 5
FINISH OFF

To finish, turn the storage dumpty the right-side out and fill with toys, fabric, yarn – whatever you need to tidy up!

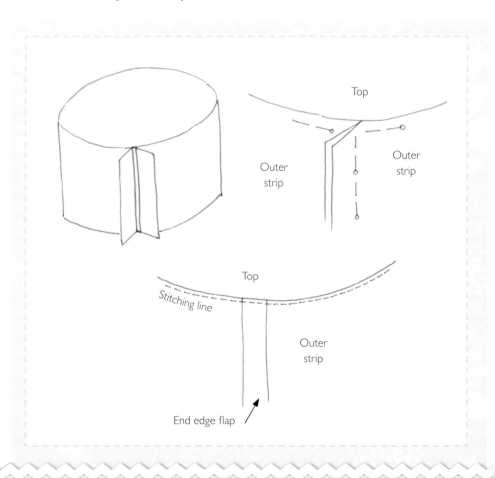

Scrappy Quilt

This pretty quilt is a great way to use up those small pieces of fabric in your stash.

About this Pattern

1 ●○○○○ Beginner

Step 1

MAKE BLOCKS

Place a medium square in the top-right corner of a large square and sew into place, approx 0.5cm (²/₈in) from the edge. Place a small square on top, in the top-right corner of the medium square and sew into place approx 0.5cm (²/₈in) from the edge.

Step 2

JOIN BLOCKS

Join four blocks together as shown in the diagram. Repeat these two steps until all your squares have been used.

MATERIALS

18 fat quarters of fabric to make all the blocks for the front of the quilt. You can cut all small squares from two fat quarters or equivalent. You will need 2.25m (87in) of fabric for the back.
Wadding
Thread for quilting

CUTTING LIST

Large squares – cut 36 measuring approx 25cm (10in) square

Medium squares – cut 36 measuring approx 12cm (5in) square

Small squares – cut 36 measuring approx 6cm (2.5in) square

FINISHED SIZE

110cm x 153cm (43in x 60in)

PATTERN NOTES

We used half green, half blue-based fabric for the medium squares and arranged the blocks so the same colours were diagonally opposite each other. The edges of the blocks are intended to be unfinished. You can cut squares using a rotary cutter, or scissors if you don't mind the squares and blocks being slightly different sizes.

Step 3
COMPLETE QUILT TOP

Join the large blocks together in rows, as shown in the diagram.

Step 4
BACKING

Cut your backing fabric to the correct size – it needs to measure approximately 7.5cm (3in) bigger than the quilt top all the way around. Lay it face down on a flat surface and tape into place.

Step 5
PIN QUILT

Place the wadding on top of the back of the quilt, then place the quilt top face up on top of the wadding. Pin into place.

Step 6
QUILT AND BIND

Quilt then bind the quilt using your preferred method.

Top Tip
Choose fabric patterns that create interesting three-dimensional effects when you layer them.

Scrappy Cushions

A great project for all those little pieces of fabric you might have in your stash.

About this Pattern

1 ●●○○○ Beginner

Step 1

CUT AND JOIN FABRIC SCRAPS

Cut your scraps of fabric into rectangles and squares as per the cutting list. Join the rectangles together three at a time to form a block as shown in the photo (right). Join nine of the squares together to form a block as shown in the photo (right).

Step 2

JOIN BLOCKS INTO STRIPS.

Join four of the blocks of squares together to form one strip. Repeat with the remaining four blocks. Join four of the blocks of rectangles together to form one strip, turning them so that they are a mixture of horizontal and vertical stripes.

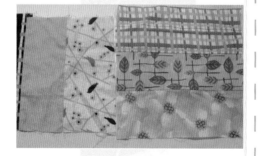

MATERIALS

Cushion front: oddments of fabric.

Cushion back: 1m (1yd) of complementary fabric.

Matching thread

71cm (28in) cushion insert

FINISHED SIZE

Cushion cover is approx. 76cm (30in) square, to fit a cushion pad of approx 71cm (28in).

CUTTING LIST

From the scraps of fabric:

24 x rectangles measuring 25cm x 8cm (10in x 3in)

72 x squares measuring 8cm x 8cm (3in x 3in)

From the back fabric:

2 pieces measuring 76cm x 50cm (30in x 20in)

SEAM ALLOWANCE:

1cm (¼in) throughout

PATTERN NOTES

You can also make the back of the cushion from fabric scraps if you have enough, or use two different pieces of fabric for each side.

Step 3

JOIN STRIPS TOGETHER.

Join the four strips together to form a
square shape. Don't worry too much if the
fabrics do not match up entirely or if your
blocks are slightly different shapes.
This will only add to the charm of your
scrappy cushion.

Step 4

JOIN CUSHION FRONT TO BACK

Take the pieces of backing fabrics that
you have cut and hem 1.5cm (½in) around
all four sides. Lay one of the pieces down,
right-sides together, with the patched
cushion front and sew together along
three sides. Repeat with the other backing
piece. The backing pieces will overlap
each other as you are sewing them – this
allows for you to put the cover on the
cushion.

Step 5

FINISH

Turn right
side out.
Press and
insert
cushion pad.

Top Tip

You could use either
all rectangle strips
or all square strips,
depending on the size
of your scraps.

Tie-dye
Beanbag

A unique addition to any teen's bedroom. First, dye the fabric – choose your dyes to coordinate with your décor.

Step 1
CUT PANEL

Before you start, wash and dry the cotton fabric, then cut a square about 80cm x 80cm (31½in x 31½in).

Step 2
TIE FABRIC

Lay the fabric square on a tabletop. Find the centre of the square (do this by folding into quarters) and pinch the centre between your thumb and forefinger. Start to turn your hand and twist the fabric. It will fold in on itself and form a spiral. Keep twisting until all of the fabric has been drawn into the spiral and you have a bundle roughly circular in shape, if any of the pleats are too high, fold them down. Secure the bundle with elastic bands – you'll need at least three. Make sure all the ends are tucked in so the bundle is tight.

Step 3
PREPARE FABRIC

Put on the plastic gloves, and soak the tied panel for half an hour in a sink full of hot water and soda ash. We recommend filling the sink about half full and using about ¾ cup soda ash. After half an hour, squeeze the excess water out of the bundle (taking care not to upset the arrangement of the folds), and place on a table which you have covered in thick plastic bags.

Step 4
DYE FABRIC

Making sure to wear the gloves, mix your dyes. Put about 2.5 teaspoons of dye in a squeezy bottle, then fill the bottle up about ¾ of the way. Shake and make sure the dye is blended thoroughly. Mix up at least three different colours to make an effective spiral.

Step 5
WASH

The next day, untie your bundle, and unfold it in the sink, rinsing under the tap. When the water is running relatively clear, put the fabric into the washing machine, and wash it with detergent (on its own, or with other tie-dyed stuff) at least 60 degrees. When your fabric has dried, it will be ready to use.

MAKE PATTERN: To make the spiral pattern – Make a triangle with the point in the middle of the spiral. Repeat with the other colours and alternate triangle sections. Repeat on the back of the bundle. The dyes will run into each other so don't worry. Squirt the dye into the folds of the fabric – this will give a greater colour intensity on your finished panel. Now leave the dyed bundle overnight.

FINISHED SIZE
Circumference - approx 238cm

MATERIALS
Woven cotton (quilting weight) in white or cream - 1m
Bin bags
Soda ash
3 different colours of dye
Rubber bands
Thin plastic gloves
Squeezy bottles with nozzles

PATTERN NOTES
These instructions make a large beanbag – about the same size (perhaps slightly bigger) as a standard bag. You can very easily adjust the measurements to make a smaller or larger one, or a cushion.
The quantities of dye given below normally dye about 4-5 items. Since you have to get out all your bin bags and rubber gloves anyway, why not do a t-shirt or old pillowcase at the same time? Of course, you can also halve the dye quantities.

Sew Beanbag

A colourful addition to any teen's bedroom.
Once you have dyed your fabric, it's time to sew!

About this Pattern

1 ●○○○○ Beginner

Step 1
CUT FABRIC

Out of the square tie-dyed fabric, cut a circle that is 76cm (30in) across. The easiest way to do this is to put a pin in the centre of the square (this will be obvious as it's a spiral), and measure 38cm (16in) all round at points about 7cm (2¾in) apart, marking with chalk. This will be enough for you to draw a circle. When you have cut out your circle, fold it into quarters to check that the top edge is even. Trim as necessary.

Step 2
CUT BEANBAG BOTTOM

Fold this circle in half and use it as a template to cut out the bottom of the beanbag from the 1m (1yd) of fabric.

Step 3
PIECE TOGETHER

For a 76cm (30in) circle, you will need to make a strip 238cm (93¾in) long plus a 1cm (⅛in) seam allowance. Aim to make a strip about 245cm (96½in), which will give you room for error. Choose a selection of fabrics which tone with the colours in the dyed panel (or contrast with it). Cut strips of different widths, all 35cm (13¾in) long. This will make your beanbag about 32cm (13in) high – if you would like it either flatter or taller just adjust the length of your strip. Allow a 1cm (⅜in) seam on your pieces. Sew your strip together and press the seams open.

STEP 4
ATTACH SIDE PANEL

Pin the right side of the strip to the right side of the top panel, being careful to keep the circle shape intact. Use this to judge how long your pieced strip needs to be (remembering the seam allowance) – sew the ends of the pieced strip so it forms a circle (being careful not to twist it). You should be able to do this without unpinning all the top panel, just the bit where the seam is. Sew the top panel to the pieced strip using a 1cm (⅜in) seam allowance. Press the seam towards the pieced strip.

Step 5
SEW TO BOTTOM

Pin and sew the strip to the bottom piece,

MATERIALS

Dyed fabric - 80cm x 80cm (31½in x 31½in)

Cotton fabric - 1m (1yd)

Assortment of scraps, 35cm (13¾in) long, enough to make a strip about 245cm (96½in) long when sewn together

Bags of beanbag beads for stuffing

PATTERN NOTES

These instructions are for a beanbag which is stuffed and then sewn closed, as this is the easiest and quickest way to do it: it will mean, however, that you can't remove the cover to wash it (or not without removing all the stuffing first). If you prefer, you can make a removable cover by following the instructions below to make an inner cushion, then sew the outer bag in exactly the same way (same measurements) but insert a zip into the bottom seam.

leaving a 26cm (10¼in) gap for stuffing. Turn the beanbag to the right side.

Step 6
STUFF

Stuff with the beanbag filling (it's easiest to use a jug and accept that you're going to have to hoover afterwards). The filling will settle a little in use so stuff quite full, but don't overstuff. Sew the gap closed and your beanbag is ready.

Top Tip

You can mix colours of dyes – feel free to experiment – but if this is your first attempt it might be easier to use them as they come.

Simple Throw

This cosy throw would be perfect on a bed or chair or even used as a blanket for a summer picnic.

About this Pattern

1 ⬤○○○○ Beginner

Step 1
TRIM FLEECE

Cut your fleece blanket to the exact size given in the materials list.

Step 2
CUT COTTON FABRIC

Cut your cotton fabric into 4 strips that measure 5cm (2in) wide and are longer than the length of your fleece blanket by 24cm (10in).

Step 3
PRESS COTTON FABRIC

Fold the strips of cotton fabric in half lengthways. Press. Unfold the strips and turn the raw long edges 2cm (³/₄in) to the inside. Press each turn. Repeat with all 4 strips.

Step 4
ATTACH COTTON STRIPS

Take the first cotton strip and pin into place along one of the sides of your fleece blanket. Ensure that the pressed edge in the middle of the strip is comfortably against the edge of the blanket. Hand sew into place on both sides. Repeat for opposite side of blanket.

Step 5
PREPARE FINAL STRIPS

Take the 2 final strips and turn the short edges in by 2.5cm (1in) each end. Press to form a neat edge.

Step 6
ATTACH FINAL STRIPS

Sew the final 2 strips to the fleece blanket ensuring that the edges are neat.

MATERIALS

Fleece blanket measuring 140cm x 100cm (55in x 40in)

250cm (98in) cotton fabric

Matching thread

Sewing needle

Pins

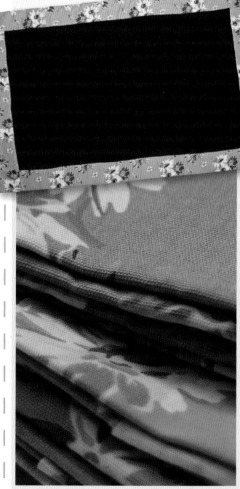

Scrappy Napkin

Use up those small pieces of fabric you have leftover to make these almost-matching napkins – perfect for dinner parties!

About this Pattern

1 ⬤○○○○ Beginner

MATERIALS

Scraps of fabric measuring a total of approx. 30cm x 20cm (12in x 8in) for each side of each napkin

Pinking sheers

Contrasting thread

FINISHED SIZE

Each napkin measures approx. 30cm x 20cm (12in x 8in). If you make them slightly different sizes, you'll have a more eclectic collection!

Step 1
CHOOSE YOUR FABRICS

Choose the fabrics that you are going to use for your first napkin and join the scraps together to measure approx 30cm x 20cm (12in x 8in). Repeat to prepare a second side for your napkin using other scraps.

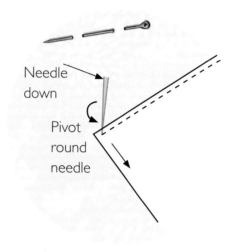

Needle down

Pivot round needle

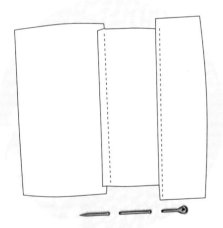

Step 2
JOIN TOGETHER

With wrong-sides together, sew around your two pieces of fabric, approx 1.5cm (⅝in) from the edge, using a contrasting thread. When it comes to the corners, move your needle to the down position and turn the napkin so that you can sew neatly without any movement of the stitches.

Step 3
EDGING

Using pinking sheers, cut close to the line of contrast stitching, leaving approx 0.5cm (⅛in) between the stitching and the edge of the napkins. This gives a decorative finish to your napkin.

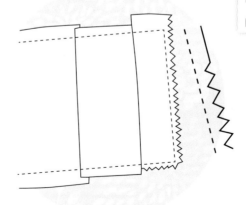

Step 4
OPTIONAL EXTRAS

These napkins are a great way to experiment with new fabric collections or to use up scraps of fabric. They can be embellished using buttons, ribbon, ric-rac or anything else you have available.

Simple Apron

Made from just two tea towels, this apron
is stylish and simple to make.

Step 1
SEW TEA TOWELS TOGETHER

Take both tea towels and lay them
together right sides facing out. Sew
around three of the edges approx.
1cm (¼in) from the edge, just inside
the seam of the tea towels.

Step 2
PREPARE STRAPS

Cut two pieces of fabric measuring 65cm
(25in) by 1cm (2in). Fold in half, neaten
the edge and sew along the long side.

Step 3
ATTACH STRAPS

Sew the straps, one either side, of the top
of the apron.

MATERIALS

- White sewing thread
- 2 x tea towels
- Either a third tea towel for ties or
  piece of material measuring 10cm
  (4in) by 65cm (25in)

Patchwork
Table Runner

Table runners can be beautifully quilted or embellished. This one uses scraps of fabric to create a stylish look for your kitchen table.

About this Pattern

1 ●○○○○ Beginner

MATERIALS

Scraps of fabric measuring a total of approx 30cm x 150cm (12in x 20in) for each side of your table runner

Pinking sheers

Contrasting thread

FINISHES

30cm x 144cm (12in x 59in)

Step 1

CHOOSE YOUR FABRICS

Choose the fabrics that you are going to use for your table runner and join your scraps together in a long length, which measures 30cm x 144cm (12in x 57in). Prepare a second side for your table runner using other scraps. We used pieces of fabric that were all 30cm (12in) wide but were different lengths – if you choose to use smaller pieces of fabric, your table runner will have a more patchwork feel to it.

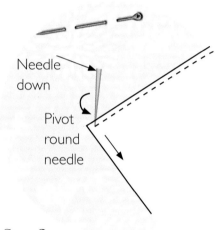

Needle down

Pivot round needle

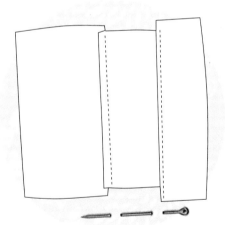

Step 2

JOIN TOGETHER

With wrong sides together, sew around your two pieces of fabric, approx 1.5cm (¹⁄₈in) from the edge, using contrasting thread. When it comes to the corners, move your needle to the down position and turn the table runner so that you can sew neatly without any movement of the stitches.

Step 3

EDGING

Using the pinking shears, cut close to the line of contrast stitching, leaving approx 0.5cm (²⁄₈in) between the stitching and the edge of the table runner. This gives a decorative finish.

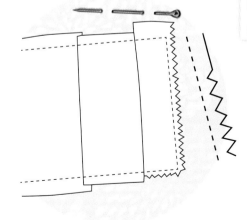

Step 4

OPTIONAL EXTRAS

Your table runner is now ready to be embellished using buttons, ribbon, ric-rac or anything else that you want to sew on to personalise it. You could sew ribbon at most of the fabric changes, to highlight the movement of the fabrics, or add beads or buttons to the edge of your runner, or use two very different colourways on either side of the runner for two looks in one!